The Last Bridge Is Home

# The Last Bridge Is Home

Poems by

Rodd Whelpley

Cover design by Shay Culligan

ISBN: 978-1-954353-52-7

Kelsay Books
502 South 1040 East, A-119
American Fork, Utah, 84003

# Acknowledgments

My thanks to the editors of these journals where the following poems (or earlier versions of them) first appeared:

*8 Poems:* "Agoraphobia"
*Antiphon:* "Twenty years" (originally untitled)
*Barren Magazine:* "How do you call it when"
*Black Napkin Press:* "1981" (originally "Twins. 1981. Nowhere, Ohio")
*Catch as Kitsch Can* (Prolific Press, 2018): "The Secret Kingdom of the Twins," "My dog feigns he's new to English," "The day you are married"
*Chagrin River Review:* "My Dad Forgets"
*Elysian Fields Quarterly:* "Going to a New Ballpark"
*Emerge literary Journal:* "Leavings"
*Ghost City Review:* "Lido"
*Likely Red:* "The Thing that Would Make her Happy"
*Menacing Hedge:* "My dog feigns he's new to English," "A Pocket Guide to Native Tongues"
*Pif:* "The Gray Anniversary" (originally "Consider the Rain")
*Rockvale Review:* "The Spaceman"
*Star 82 Review:* "The day we are married" (originally "The day you are married")
*The Broadkill Review:* "A house," "The Giraffe is a Friendly Animal"
*The Ear:* "Your Wife Decides on Kayaks"
*The Shore:* "Something about a bridge"
*Tinderbox Poetry Journal:* "Someone Else's Car"

# Notes

"The Thing that Would Make her Happy" borrows phrases and images from the following poems:

"Thirteen Ways of Looking at a Blackbird" by Wallace Stevens: "I know noble accents / And lucid, inescapable rhythms."

"Paterson" by William Carlos Williams: "No ideas but in things."

"The Waste Land" by T.S. Eliot: "I will show you fear in a handful of dust."

"After Apple Picking" by Robert Frost: "For all / That struck the earth, / No matter if not bruised or spiked with stubble, / Went surely to the cider-apple heap / As of no worth."

*Image Credit:*

The free-to-use covered bridge artwork for part opening pages comes from All Things Clipart (http://www.allthingsclipart.com/covered.bridges.clipart.htm).

*Special Thanks:*

To Richie Hofmann for his early and unstinting encouragement and to Madeleine Corley for her patient and sharp criticism of early drafts of this manuscript and the many suggestions that improved this chapbook.

# Contents

# Front Piece

*In Ashtabula County, Ohio, stand 18 covered bridges, including the longest and shortest in the United States.*

*There were not quite so many—only 13—in the early 1970s when my twin brother Ryan would beg our father to take us driving. Ryan liked bridges. Dad liked his Oldsmobile, and I didn't like or understand either thing but went along for the ride.*

*We'd feel the car bumpity bump as its tires bounced from the end of a wooden bridge back to a hardtop lane. Immediately Ryan would plead, "One more. One more bridge." And my father would turn the car towards the next span. Until, after a crossing way south, he would say to us, "The last bridge is home," and take us north, toward Lake Erie, and our slate gray foursquare at 288 West Liberty in our hometown of Geneva.*

*These trips were the one thing Ryan and my father shared, or thought they shared. I could never tell if they were ignorant or if they knew—and just chose to ignore—that my father thought we were out for a drive, and my brother hoped we were crossing the bridges—all the bridges, especially the last.*

* * * * *

*Ryan, this little book is for you, your whole life singing from a riverbank on which you should never have stood alone. Years ago, I left to try to make a different home, a more accepting, less silent family.*

*But I hear you, still.*

*I promise.*

# Part 1

Brother ~ Son

# The Secret Kingdom of the Twins

That 1970s Camelot. Upstairs alliance
of the boys' rooms—*Sound of Music* Austria

and *Sound of Music* Switzerland—arteried
by a walk-through closet, a mountain pass,

for smuggles in war, shadow kisses
in war and peace. Our little guys,

his Brownie bear, my single-eyed Ton Ton;
His Suzie bear and my Raggedy Andy,

who were lovers, resistant, brave-facing the blitz,
sorties of plastic TWA bombers,

faceless enemies fighting up the steps, dispatched,
perhaps, by hand-wrung aunts or parents,

concerned how all the names and voices
of his animals are girls. Of course they were.

Because, after every war, a parade and wedding
to the album-version of *March of the Siamese Children*—

Andy decorated with dad's lost button,
Suzie, tissues pinned to drape below her snout—

a progress through Mirabell Gardens' arch of men
past Pegasus Fountain to the thrones

of King César and Queen Violet Bear, who would knight
and unite them: The end of every good story,

me strategizing the next day's battle,
my brother impossible dreaming a veiled place for us,

where Tony could at last forsake Maria,
meet my brother's eyes, make his name a song.

# Going to a New Ballpark

When I ascend the ramp, see the field
with no one out there,
it's the way I pictured it
at five O'clock some summer afternoons
when father would come home from the shop.
He'd park the Olds in the drive,
and, as he'd walk toward the house,
Scot or Dinky or Dave or I would wave him over
to the empty lot that was
Fenway, Comiskey, Wrigley or the Stick.

Without yelling in to mother,
he'd drop his lunchbox on the stoop,
come to us;
Dinky would call him all-time pitcher,
and the game, sometimes hours old,
would begin.

So now, when I see the new-mown grass,
the dragged infield, the fresh-chalked base paths,
I see the game how it was and how it's going to be
until the home team scrambles from the dugout
and takes position.

It's silly, I know,
but, just once,
I want the man
who kicks the rubber, digs the mound,
and whips a few warm up curves at the catcher
to pitch nine good innings
to both sides—

And wear dad's steel-toed shoes.

# The Giraffe Is a Friendly Animal

I have this on the highest authority—
my twin brother when we were five
at a visit to the Cleveland Zoo. And cows

pinch grandpa's chew-tobacc, but never
spit it out. Birds sometimes fall in love
with jumbo jets—always a disaster. Circus

peanuts we toss to monkey island
replicate the diet of colobus inmates taken
from the wild. The elephant never forgets

our names and what we wore last year.
In the ape house, you can feed a machine.
Two quarters, and a blue gorilla will pop out.

In the hot car home, its plastic face will melt,
but Dad will not complain about the money.
And mom won't cry today. When they think

we are asleep, they'll say, Five years. How can it be
five years? Human grownups think that speed
is magic. That five years old doesn't last forever.

# The Change Game

She tried explaining to us why she was exhausted
and not too proud to say it, why red marks butterflied her face,
but we'd never been treated like adults before. So all we learned
from mom is lupus stands for wolf in doctor talk,
which is why my brother and I each month waited at the clinic,
both with a handful of dirty coins, gifts from our father
(in the exam room with mom) and a game:
                                    One by one, show
the nickels, dimes, quarters; make each other guess their dates—
years before our births—a non-disturbing way to kill the time
alone while our parents talked to someone called a specialist,
who would tell our mother to stay away from sun, switch
to low-tar cigarettes, the days to take more prednisone and ones—
we all prepared for—to take a little less.
                                    We learned the trick
for reckoning change was judging grime on eagle wings, or scars
on Jefferson's face from friction with dad's pocket knife. And
when we'd arrived correctly at the date of every one, we left,
followed the yellow line painted on the floor that would take us
to a vending machine, where once, indecisive about candy,
we irked a looming white-coat doctor, who scolded us
with hungry snarls and sighs.
                                    We stepped aside. Still,
he demanded what were we doing here. My brother said, Mom
has the Red Wolf living deep inside her. The doctor set his lips,
gathered his Pepsi and jellyfish, hurried away. Like a predator,
I sighted him as he tapped an orderly, nodded at us, muttered
'unsupervised,' as a synonym for hate. I wonder.
                                    Did he notice
my teeth and nails whet? My guard hairs rise? The monster
in my mother transfiguring inside me? I know he heard—
as did they all—when I pierced the Cleveland Clinic din
with my desperate, gamey, howling.

# Agoraphobia

We wasted our twinness;
     Knew it even then.

Did not harmonize
     the six-four-three double play

or hit the close chords, become
     the next Don and Phil Everly.

Did not develop a secret way
     of speaking.

So at thirteen, I knew you
     only at the piano

from each morning's Sonata Pathétique,
     your tempo, the pedaling,

the weight of your arms held
     like a crimped torrent, or else

sound sliding from your fingertips
     natural as water drops on a glass.

Words in our house
     (how often we were reminded)

were expensive. The doctor—
     beyond the deductible—

to call this thing of yours
     a condition

with a name—The fear
        of leaving a safe place.

You must choose a between home
        with a stack of Beethoven and

no one brave to whisper the unpleasant—
        to even ask a question; or else

face junior high locker banks: Kicks and fists to the tune
        of 'sissy,' 'queer' and 'fag.'

Mornings, after mom and dad have gone for work,
        after breakfast, brushing, packing—

inside the front door you collapse.
        There, your voiceless crying

leaves space for the swing and click
        of the Regulator clock,

time on your side,
        like measures falling

to that caesura where neither—
        or just one of us—must go to school.

You make me step around you,
        sometimes overtop you.

Then down the street I backpedal,
        see you, at the window, watching me.

I want our gaze to break.
      Let me imagine you—

your perfect preludes and fugues of Bach—
      all day in every key. But you only stare,

when we both know, in movies
      this is when

you'd snatch your books, run
      to meet me, or else

as I turn and walk away,
      throw open the pane,

take to the piano, ring the neighborhood
      with the sound of our fraternity,

launch me away on something flawless—
      perhaps the Rhapsody in Blue.

# Someone Else's Car

My mother's legs are filthy.
She is sun browned and dirt browned,
the sweat gluing dust and clippings
in rivulet patterns on her face, neck, arms.
She has cut the grass, then
quietly weeded the back flower garden,
stretched on her side, like a cat
daydreaming things you wouldn't dare to know.
Beside her, she's arranged a colander, filled,
roots and all, with curly docks.
A single line of turned earth and Carlton butts
points back to where she's been.

To listen to me, she has stabbed her putty knife
at parade rest into the ground before
a deliberate row of soldier-straight polyanthus.
Seeing her, I see now how no one ever loved
the solace of the dirt like my mother.
And I, newly licensed, have stopped her
with my blather about a classic sputnik car
at a used lot on Route 20. I say the words
beautiful, spotless, tiny and like new. Though
I suspect I'm speaking at the empty air,
to answer me, she smartly thumps the ground. Says,
Goddamn. We've got to drive it.

Scrubbed, censored by Lifebuoy and Arpège,
we present ourselves at closing time.
The shaggy salesman wants to go,
wants to say so without words, tilts his head,
scratches, like a flea bit dog, at his neck,
while my mom describes perfectly a car she's never seen.
Metropolitan, he says, A later one.
Sold it today. Guy'll pick her up tomorrow.

He's too relieved he can head for home.
There's a moment of no talking, but
my mother can say something,
standing slender, tall and silent in a summer dress.

He backs it out the bay, a two-tone compact
for the Eisenhower age. Creaks open the door.
We cannot drive someone else's car. But see it? Sure.
He leaves us alone on the fabric bench with vinyl trim.
My mother, unlike me, does not look fearful at the clutch.
She takes the wheel with grace. Hers now, this old car
that rolled off the line when she was twenty-eight
and married near a dozen years with a kid as old as that,
and others bound to come. Then, she couldn't imagine
this, styled for a family that could think of second vehicles,
or for a college girl, the one she never got to be,
packing light for Florida to discover where the boys are.

The Metropolitan sits, like a frost berry white
and Berkshire green stanza wrenched upon a page.
Mom's hand brushes slowly along the three on the tree.
We have no keys. But we have ignition.
Her lips move soundlessly,
forming perhaps meanings for words like
beautiful, spotless, tiny and new. I see mother
seem other than either of us has ever known,
see her, in that last instant unencumbered,
driving all the unmapped routes there ever were,
on pavement where we both agree
it's OK I don't exist.

# 1981

After those kid years sleeping together—
you, my brother, and I huddled

in the bottom bunk, children rocking,
pretending we were riding with Hercule Poirot

on the Orient Express—why now
seventeen, drunk, kicked out of the drive-in,

lying in our (finally) separate rooms
across a hallway, doors open, do I at last

feel your breath, when you whisper
across the gap, how, today—fourth period,

you kissed Frank, the first-chair trumpet,
in the darkness of the practice room?

The most reverberant *forte / pianissimo* ever
in this house. And our windows did not shatter.

# Part 2

Husband ~ Father
Brother ~ Son

# The day we are married,

not the one we were wed,
surfaces like a white
porpoise on the Baltic Sea.

A night beneath the sheets,
we challenge each other:
Recall the lyrics of an offhand tune.
And, it's as understood as it is unsaid

the bride will affect the boy howdy
and the timbre of 1970s Glen Campbell.
Belt that *Rhinestone Cowboy*. Paste
its echo to every corner of our home.

# My dog feigns he's new to English,

pretends these fat, ant-ridden buds
bursting from starts we rescued years ago
from the gardens at my boyhood
home, my wife's family's century farm

are called pee-on-mees. And I say
"No, Buster, peonies. *Peonies.*" And he
stares blankly, evincing not a bit
of sorrow that he's sopped in ammonia

and uric acid a hundred years
of plowing, sowing, of hoping for work,
of whispers—the dark lady unnamed
in the margins of photos, the uncle light

in the loafers, the brother too, the money
absconded—secrets, as cold as those beers
hidden in the toilet tank, meetings
with that social worker ending

in silences harder than a slap.
Pissed so cavalierly on those roots
we carefully dug from the clay of Ohio,
the soil of Iowa to replant to this backyard

in another state, a plot on which we hope
to grow some better flower. He pees
and pees on the peonies that come spring
refuse to do a thing. Except they bloom.

# Twenty years

                    and a child later,
she sleeps on the opposite shore of the wet spot,
a shallow body between us we've come
to respect.

On the terrain of our sheets
this is lake size.

I lie at the latitude of Toledo,
a city of glass.
She is Toronto,
familiar and foreign.

The third grade teacher said
Erie—by volume—is the smallest of the Great Lakes,
a strange thing to tell a boy in Ohio.

That summer,
in to my waist,
I squinted against the light stippling off the waves
my sights to the horizon,
straining, even then, for Canada.

# Something about a bridge

that each time you cross,
you look down, unsure the water
will still be there.
Or else as if to gauge whether today
the pool finally swelled
to leaping depth, for falling
to what end you never know.
God didn't trouble these waters.
People did, upstream,
choking the flow,
leaving here inches—
barely atmosphere
for Jesus bugs
and crayfish.

Like those living
under that other bridge,
a different creek, the water
you caressed, moving a stone
but not its mud, revealing him.
Insinuated your hands below the surface,
perching one abaft, the other in front,
then closing like a stern curtain
before his eyestalk, his flailing
antenna, until that champion
of backward propulsion shot
into the gentle hand behind,
which he had no sense to sense.

Today, in the thinning trickle
sit shadows of things thrown over:
a set of tires, a Remington—
typewriter, not a gun—
the refuse of ways
those before you
tried to go. And also,
as under every bridge,
that unseen old crustacean
you once held, a pet
in your childish grasp.

# The Spaceman

If I were the new Neil Armstrong,
my craft sling-shot past the moon,
in transit or, perhaps, in orbit,
mapping ice lochs, finding purchase

for settling on the light side
of Proxima b,
I'd do for you that
anti-gravity shtick, flipping,

flying through my capsule,
floating toothpaste out the tube—
Apollo old-school stuff
broadcast in high-def to your phone

almost like you'd be with me.
Maybe just as good.
Imagine it: Me, your dad,
perfect on paper,

but a failure
on the earth-bound plane
now a voyager, mission-ready,
laughing at your laughter

of my pinwheel, sleeper,
walk the dog—tricks impossible
on solid ground, now accomplished
with airless ease,

missives
from me, your different father,
yo-yoing the exoplanet
closest to a different sun.

Both of us delighted
at the smallest provocation,
as if weightless were a way
that we could be.

# The Thing That Would Make Her Happy

I know the thing that would make her happy
is if I would use a word from the chart
posted on her office wall. I see it
when I look away from the perfect lipstick
of her social work smile or her eyes that,
pupil-to-pupil, pin to mine while she
waits the silent prelude of an answer.

I know such noble accents and lucid,
inescapable rhythms (carry them
useful as birdhouses into courtrooms),
but won't make space for her eight small words, paired
in two columns, that you'd think—if they were
essential—would have at birth, or at least
by now, double helixed somewhere in me.

I want to say there are no ideas
but in things. The thing where I smacked my kid.
The thing where I eat the candy until
my hands quiver. The thing where I can't keep
details of the trauma that left these scars.
She wants me to say, yes, these are some things,
say there are also things *not* ideas.

As if I cannot cast handfuls of dust.
I have for years, dispelling notions like

| Fear | Anger |
|---------|-------|
| Pain | Joy |
| Passion | Love |
| Guilt | Shame |

Words that I can toss on the cider heap,
or which hang fixed to that chart, not at all
like a ring of keys, but like some structure.
House frame. Window pane. The scaffolding of
a stanza for a person I don't know.

# The One That Starts with 'A'

*(1999 and two decades later)*


In tune with your four p.m. snores
      pitched perfect from the bedroom, I stare
ignorant how your living room carpet, swept smooth,
resembles a fallow field in Clear Lake, Iowa.
      I wait for you to wake, bundle you
against the Florida sun in winter,
      an outing to the Melting Pot, another chance
to astonish a waitress that we,
at least a little longer—like Louie De Palma
      and the Terminator—are twins.
You hadn't the room to get thinner,
      but you did. I expect they'll have to safety pin

your jacket for the visitation,
      which may be easier for us both
than this farewell tour of your house,
where you sneak into my luggage
      a cassette of your senior piano recital
with an orchestra behind you and your favorite
      Gumby, Pokey, Peewee Herman tchotchkes.
In the family, only you and I
have ever said the *G*-word. Now we say
      the one that starts with *A*, but we skip
the one with *D*. As if a T-cell count of nine
      is any different from a plane crash.

                *

But that shows what I know because
      this year will now be twenty since diagnosis day.
When you call, there will be much
not to talk about: *G*ay, and *A*ids, and *D*eath. And how if I knew
      that night I would get the things for which I prayed,

40

I would have asked for more.

      How we discovered fondue is impossible
with medicine-quivered hands, also
that evil reminiscence of dad's favorite
      *Claire de Lune,* which, when you were ten,
you'd abruptly cease whenever he stepped in.
      'You'll be sad,' he said, 'When you play it

at my funeral.' To which you always said, 'I won't.'—
      The one thing we got right that night. Now,
when we speak, I picture the palsied vibrato
of the cell phone on your ear, two decades of tremors
      that make a misadventure of finding middle C.
Remember when we drove back home
      how we cranked the A.M. station,
sang 'bye bye' so loud to all of Tampa—
Every word of that song by Don McLean
      about three men who missed composing fates
for those who crashed but somehow did survive
      the day their music died.

# A Pocket Guide to Native Tongues

Words can't capture the nuance of anything
precisely because they are mole traps
    with invisible springs.

Seasons neatly colored.
*Geegaw Geegaw Geegaw*
    My baby used to sing.

It meant summer. It meant winter. It meant
fall, and a decline without declension, as if
    geegaw wasn't a verb.

Which it is. And a noun, and also
adjectival: The description of a song.
    The songbird.

And the singing, sailing for the un-ambitted space
where a childish nothing finds, at last, the edge
    of everything.

# Your Wife Decides on Kayaks

Put in at the turnout past the S-curve. Then
she'll choose the lake or its feeder creek.

You'll follow across the cove, slip with her
between the banks, trees above, their arms stretched

for leafy partners on the other side
like the arch of a Virginia Reel,

your boats, a shy, un-touching couple
passing underneath. Soft whiffs of stillness

slowly outdo the cold, wet-fur odor
of deeper water. Red-dappled snakes wishing

they were copperheads stop sunning, join you
in the calm, cause wakes as wide as yours.

Pterodactyl herons sail the wind, angry,
grocking that your paddle strokes awoke turtles

they'd stalked since sunrise. This much life
on this small body, a moment to remind you:

Dying is easy—a hundred percent success
in the history of us, save biblical exceptions

with which you do not hold. Still, you follow
though you suspect she knows the way

even less than you. Faith is not a stream
that never dips and shallows on the rocks.

It ripples on—to you, the boat ahead,
the love who sits there, the buoyancy of now.

# My Dad Forgets

My dad forgets.
Forgets he has already shown us my mother's grave.
Forgets my son's name, calls him sometimes
by mine, taps his head, asks the old question:
"Do you play ball, son?" He shows us
the tennis ball, softball, golf ball he's placed on
my mother's grave: A custom at the new cemetery in our town.
Later, he soft tosses a Titleist he's found on a headstone.
"Aint that crazy?" he asks. Then says, "Nice catch.
Do you play ball, son?"

My dad forgets.
Forgets he has already eaten one lunch today.
Forgets this morning we have visited the old cemetery,
where his wife is not, but his mother is.
He can't say why his father is not buried
by his mother—some circumstance I never knew
and won't. My father cannot find the grave
of his father, convinced it's near the plots
of his dead in laws. How that would be,
he can't say why.

My dad forgets.
Forgets he is surly, unappealing, offensive in his approaches.
Forgets these people, in this town he has lived in his whole life
are different people than he thinks have remained in this town
his whole life. They do not think of him
as the second baseman, the high school quarterback,
the happy-go-lucky, who puts in the forty hours, gets a wink,
a nod, a pass; talks away his tickets because he's steady,
loyal, pays on time, has kids good enough, and has lived here
his whole life.

My dad forgets.
Forgets any story he tells; he's already told.
Forgets he puts keys beneath the matt. We've told him not to.
This is his home, he says. No one will take things from him here.
My dad wanders, squints at thumbtacked pictures in the plaster:
my mother, at 17, bathing at the lake; at 22, with her big boys
(the twins—he can't remember now—still a decade away);
or mother at 30, ready for work at a job he can't recall.
He puzzles at these new familiar vistas all around:
This is his home.

# Leavings

I don't know if leaving
  is when buds nub the branches
  or when pale colors drop
       Your apples waiting,
       unattended on a shelf
  Grudging, tacit permission
  for my mind to wander
  from duties when I write
       The boy driving alone to that college, or
  Your poring through a book's gilt pages,
  searching for those misremembered lines
       This plate of scraps from a slice
       of the cooling pie you set
       on our fully outstretched table,
       as if, indeed, company were coming.

# A house

is a thing you leave empty
most of the day, except the dog
who spits liquid on the bamboo floor,
upset the moment you depart, licks it up
then dozes everywhere but on his bed.
You don't know how you know this
as you stand beside your briefcase at the door,
keys pocketed, patting his downy head
as he huff huff huffs what you receive
as a plea for you to stay—see once yourself
how dust settles, or mid-morning light reflects
on that painting. We always come home
you tell him and wonder if he too
is thinking of his young companion
who used to return sooner than the old humans,
his car engine clatter-banging and its bass boost
shivering the window panes to wake
the dog, signal an after-school reunion,
the musk of the boy's frowzy beard and breath
when their foreheads pressed together,
the dog's name cooed in the canine's scratchy ear,
singing a sort of hymn about walking, treats,
a belly rub—and for his snout—some kisses.
The vet said dogs don't perceive what's a short time
or a long one. A brief eternity, perhaps, is something
to believe in. Your hand twists the knob. Be good,
you say to the dog and to the air.          Be good.

# How do you call it when

nothing apparently is imminent,
but the extra weight; the hair
increasingly, if not the texture,
then the hue of the bristles
in the wire brush you used
to scrape the paint from the garage
you should replace
because it leans like a stem
naked in a westerly;
your hand that, after the day's labor,
refuses to unclaw;
the flying chips landing,
freckling again your face
until the shower
makes them drop away?

I don't want a great
recapitulation. Remember
when the boy was three?
A 10 p.m. apparition
in the family room,
his non-vibrato complaints
of how he never got the grapes
we promised after he, finally,
put away those crayons,
the nightly catalogue
of bedtime wrongs
that delighted us then.

I do not want that now.
I want to know
the names of things,
even if you and I
must make them up:

for socks that have lost their grip,
but are still my favorite;
for undiscovered syllables
resident in every utterance;
our imaginary ocean;
the noticing
how next morning
the sun rises with diminished vigor.

Maybe socks
are socks, the sun the sun,
the ocean full of kisses
given and intended.
It's easy to get confused.
Words preserve us, but
they never save. Tomorrow
we will paint, whitewash
the next family's teardown project,
miss some spots,
get lazy with the trim,
in the evening drink some wine,
and say: That is good enough.

# Lido

I can never not remember water.
Never once a time I did not trust
a pool or pond or Lake Erie

to faithfully displace my weight,
welcome me like a set of cold bedsheets
growing warm and calm, familiar

as the dream wears on—the one
where breast stroking the air just higher
than my parents' arms is flying.

Every summer, mother on the beach,
oiled and brown against her doctor's orders.
On weekends father too—too skinny—

but a knife blade in the surf to catch me
on my side stroke plunge towards Ontario,
pull me back, as if a body has an undertow,

which, now, since they are gone, I realize
it has. The long sheesh after never-ending sheesh
of waves reclaiming pebbles from the shore,

calling as Demosthenes, it's time and time and time.
Each morning at the office, I float
a grain of TetraMin to my fan-tailed friend,

the lonesome king of his aquarium,
watch him steal to the surface, poise,
snap, as if predation is the only atmosphere.

Someday, we will know each other well enough.
Then, I will ask him to recount his guppy-hood,
the wild, the first time he went swimming.

# Tableau Vivant

*October 12, 1976, Ashtabula Health Center*

"Family sculpting consists of creating an arrangement, portrait, or tableau of family members placed in various physical positions that represent their relation to each other at a particular moment in time. Satir … developed the technique of family reconstruction, or spatialization of the issue, during the 1960s."

> —Luann Costa, "Family Sculpting in the Training of Marriage and Family Counselors," in *Family Counseling and Therapy Major Issues and Topics,* Robert L. Smith and Patricia Stevens-Smith, editors (1992), page 263.

Now, at stoplights, I think how we all went,
how we wondered why we all went—
Mother, Father, me and you—
when we thought we all agreed the problem
was with you

to the office of that doctor
and the lady from the county
who only let the grownups talk. They,
who were too mad or shy to say the words
I might have told them:

You should be allowed to love a boy—
You must supposed to be a girl, because
you want to love a boy,
which is the thing at home the silence said
so loud,

drowning Beethoven
and the Mozart you pounded forcefully
on the keys, like a beautiful insistence
there could really be a boy who wants
to love a boy.

All these years of traffic signals, I'm rasping
after Statuary Gardens—a therapeutic game
they made us play: Carve living statues
with the bodies of our family in the shape
that showed them right.

I picture no details of any art garden but my own,
how you were Gumby in my hands
poised at the piano. Dad, stiff, reaching
for his racquet, leaning for the door. Mom
impossible to fix

her eyes as sharp as life, her knuckles
cracking as I made her fingers point.
When they asked me, 'Where are you?' I crouched
before my work, said, 'It's like I watch them
on TV.'

The lady said, 'Hold still,' but when the doctor
aimed his Polaroid, I crayfish crawled away
to every changing light where now I chisel prayers
for absolution from the boy who loved a boy
to his twin, who—those years ago—modeled his goodbye.

# The Gray Anniversary

I can't figure the dog.
Don't see how the beta fish

for four months has survived
the ten gallons

of our sketchy water.
Don't comprehend

my friend, what he does
in the next office

the eight hours
the company owns us.

Consider, then, the rain.
The wax on these floors.

The marvel of your keys
rattling the door

each night
these many

many years.
As if you have

no better choice.
But you return

to this imperfect place,
where I will always

find you.
Because you love.

Because you're you.
Because—

it's as if
long ago

someone also whispered
in your ear

a common prophesy—
something

about home. Something
about a bridge.

# About the Author

Rodd Whelpley manages an electric efficiency program for 32 cities across Illinois and lives near Springfield. His poems have appeared in *Tinderbox Poetry Journal, Whale Road Review, Ghost City Review, Peatsmoke, The Shore, 2River View, Star 82 Review, Kissing Dynamite, Barren, Shot Glass Journal, The Naugatuck River Review, The Chagrin River Review,* and other journals. *Catch as Kitsch Can;* his first chapbook was published in 2018. Find him at www.RoddWhelpley.com.